NO MO' BROKE

**SEVEN KEYS TO FINANCIAL SUCCESS
FROM A CHRISTIAN PERSPECTIVE**

HORACE MCMILLON

McMillon Media

The opinions expressed in this manuscript are solely the opinions of the author and do not represent the opinions or thoughts of the publisher. The author has represented and warranted full ownership and/or legal right to publish all the materials in this book.

No Mo' Broke
Seven Keys to Financial Success from a Christian Perspective
All Rights Reserved.
Copyright © 2011 Horace McMillon
v1.0

No part of this book may be reproduced, stored in a retrieval system, or transmitted by any other means: electronic, mechanical, photocopying, recording, or otherwise, without prior written permission of the copyright holders.

This publication is designed to provide accurate and authoritative information with regard to the subject matter covered. This book is supplied for information purposes only. The material herein does not constitute professional advice. It is sold with the understanding that the writer and publisher are not engaged in rendering legal, accounting, or other professional advice If legal advice or other professional assistance is required, the services of a competent professional should be sought.

McMillon Media

ISBN: 978-0-578-08485-5

Library of Congress Control Number: 2011929714

PRINTED IN THE UNITED STATES OF AMERICA

Contents

Introduction 1

THE SEVEN KEYS

Key 1: Work Hard 7
Key 2: Consider the Cost 11
Key 3: Pay God First 39
Key 4: Eliminate Debt 45
Key 5: Prepare for the Unexpected 55
Key 6: Prepare for the Future 61
Key 7: Get Started Now: Stay with It 65

Introduction

I have not written this book as someone who has done everything right. Rather, just the opposite. I have made just about every kind of mistake you can make with money. I have been up to my eyeballs in credit card debt and student loan debt. I was loaded down with auto debt and was house poor. I made risky investments in a desperate attempt to get ahead of the debt. Debt was crushing me and my family. It was stealing our joy and robbing us of our peace.

Eventually the pain of those poor decisions, poor planning, and sloppy execution caused me to seek out the seven biblical and financial principles for a sound and prosperous financial life—a No Mo' Broke life.

I am a pastor who also works for a major financial services company. I am on the front lines of the current financial crisis that has swept the nation and much of the world. The material in this book has never been more needed than it is today.

Today's Crisis

- ∞ A record number of people lost their homes in 2009. That number was surpassed in 2010.

- ∞ Families are being destroyed due to financial problems: 57 percent of those divorcing list money troubles as the number-one cause.

- ∞ People are living paycheck to paycheck, buried under $10,000 of credit card debt. They are getting ripped off by predatory lenders and stuck in a cycle of debt.

- ∞ Nearly 50 percent of Americans are uncertain if they will ever have enough to retire.

Take A Look Around You

∞ We are living in the richest nation in all of recorded human history. Just about all of us live better than most royalty ever imagined.

∞ Yet, most of us have been, or are, broke. We are racked with worry and anxiety over our finances. Too many of us are slaves to debt. We perish for a lack of financial vision for ourselves and our families. No more. "No Mo' Broke." Understand the seven principles for Christian financial well-being.

God Wants Better For Us

John 10:10 states: *"The thief cometh not, but for to steal, and to kill, and to destroy: I am come that they might have life, and that they might have it more abundantly."*

Ecclesiastes 5:18 states: *"This is what I have observed to be good: that it is appropriate for a person to eat, to drink and to find satisfaction in their toilsome labor ... during the few days of life God has given them."*

The Bible is clear that God wants us to live our lives to the fullest. God wants us to find satisfaction in our work; to enjoy the fruits of our labor. God wants us to eat and drink and enjoy our families and our friends. As long as we never fail to look out and provide for the weak and vulnerable among us and put God first, God wants us to enjoy His blessings. We are only temporary custodians of God's stuff. No Mo' Broke people love God and our fellow neighbors first and foremost. Nevertheless, No Mo' Broke people desire to enjoy the gifts God has given us. Here are the seven keys.

The Seven Keys

1. Work Hard

2. Consider the Cost

3. Pay God First

4. Get Out of Debt

5. Prepare for the Unexpected

6. Prepare for the Future

7. Get Started Now & Stick with It

Key 1: Work Hard

Ecclesiastes 9:10 states: *"Whatever your hand finds to do, do it with all your might."*

Ephesians 6:7 states: *"Serve wholeheartedly, as if you were serving the Lord."*

There is no such thing as get rich quick. Our financial well-being, to a large extent, is directly dependent on what we produce and our stewardship of it. We can't expect to get full harvest with a half planting. We must strive for excellence in our work, no matter how humble or exalted our positions. Become an expert, a master craftsperson. Develop your skills. Always be getting better. We must make ourselves invaluable in our service.

Scissors and a Paper Sack

My grandmother, Lena V. Williams, had no more than an 8th-grade education, married as a teen, had 9 children, and divorced when she was in her forties. Sounds like the makings of a blues tune, doesn't it? It wasn't. She worked for herself, owned her own home, always paid her tithes, and nearly always had the money to help her children and grandchildren who made more money than she ever dreamed of making.

How did she do it? My grandmother took pride in her work. A big part of her success was her incredible work ethic. She always said that if she had no more than a pair of scissors and a paper sack, she would make money cutting grass before she would beg. She refused to be a victim. She took agency for herself and her life.

Take Pride in Yourself

Lena V. Williams took pride in herself. Even when she was just going out to clean other folks' houses, she always took the time to fix her hair and do her makeup. To top it all off, she did all her work while wearing high heels.

Maybe the world saw her as a poor, undereducated Black woman. But that is **not** the way she saw herself.

Have Purpose for Your Work

Lena V. Williams had a purpose for her work. She wanted to own her own house, take care of her own family, and have some of the nicer things in life. She traveled the country and gave generously to those around her. It is easier to work hard when one has a clear purpose for doing so.

Key 2: Consider the Cost

Understanding How Money Works

Luke 14:28–29 states: *"Suppose one of you wants to build a tower. Won't you first sit down and estimate the cost to see if you have enough money to complete it? For if you lay the foundation and are not able to finish it, everyone who sees it will ridicule you."*

Basic Concepts for Considering the Cost

- ∞ Time to Get a Plan

- ∞ Understanding the Real Cost of Things

- ∞ Understanding Our Financial Life Cycle

- ∞ The Power of Compound Interest

- ∞ A Good Budget

Time to Get a Plan

Everyone "out there" has a plan to get your money: the clothing store, the auto dealership, the bank, the credit card companies, even the grocery store. Think about it. They, very carefully, have arranged all items in the store—even at the checkout register—in order to get us to leave as much of our money with them as possible.

If everyone else has a plan to get our money, shouldn't we have a plan to *keep* our money?

Everyone Has a Plan to Get Our Money

We need to learn how to *keep* it.

Time to Learn How Money Works

Not many of us have had a class in school that really taught us how to take care of our money. There weren't any classes about how to make a **_good budget_ when I was in school**. No one showed us how much house or car _we could really afford to buy_. We weren't taught about insurance or investing. We weren't taught how to get out of debt and stay out of debt. Well, it's time to learn.

Understanding the Real Cost of Things

How many hours do I need to work to pay for this meal?

If I make $10 per hour ($20,000 per year), how many hours does it take me to pay for this $20 dinner?

Now, we may want to say 2 hours. But we forgot tax and tithes. This takes us down to $6.50 per hour. That means it takes more than 3 hours of work to pay for this dinner. However, most of us have other bills and obligations. We pay rent and transportation. After we meet our commitments in this situation, we may very well have only $2 per hour (or less) of disposable income. That is we may only have $2 (or 20 percent of our money) for every hour of work available to spend because we have other bills and obligations.

That means in the example above, we would need to work at least 10 hours to pay for this $20 meal. Is it still worth it? Maybe. But are there some other things I want more right now? Could I have a nice meal for less and get those other things? Understanding the cost allows us to make better decisions.

A better understanding makes for better decisions.

Understanding Our Financial Life Cycle

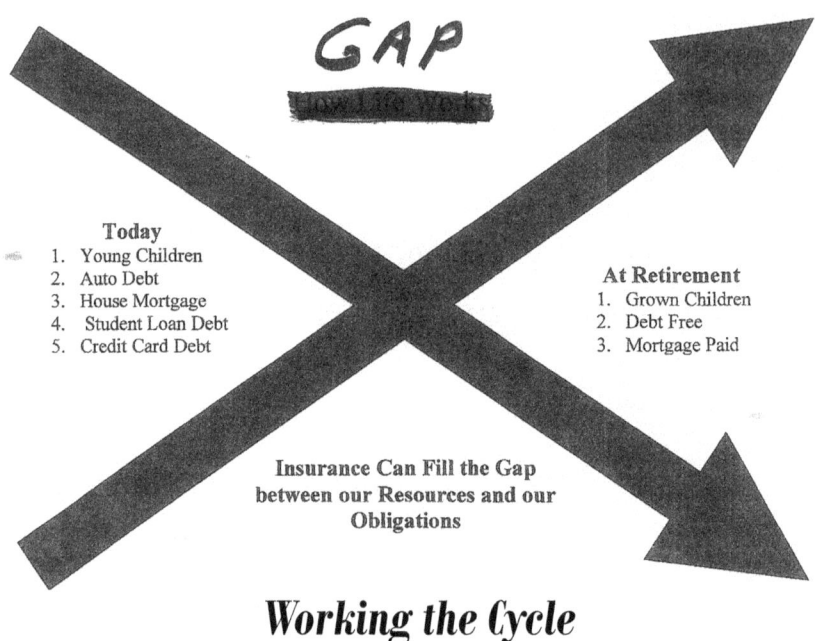

Working the Cycle

When most of us start out, we don't have a lot. We may have student loan debt, mortgage debt, auto debt, credit card debt. We often have young children for whom we need to provide. This is where insurance comes into play.

As we get older, we need to have all those debts paid down or paid off and the children grown and out. What we need is a big pile of money to provide for ourselves in the years we will not be working.

The Power of Compound Interest

- ∞ Three families work hard and save $200 per month every month for 35 years.

- ∞ The difference is that one family makes a 3 percent rate of return.

- ∞ The second family makes a 6 percent rate of return, and

- ∞ The third family makes a 12 percent rate of return.

Let's see what difference it makes.

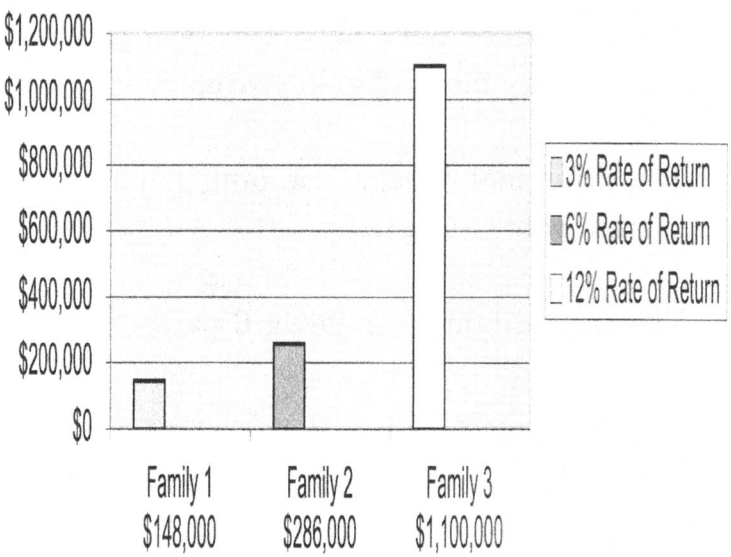

The first family investing at a 3 percent rate of return earned $148,000.

The second family saving at a 6 percent rate of return earned $186,000.

The third family saving at a 12 percent rate of return earned $1,100,000.

Same Savings, Different Accumulation!

In the last example, we saw three families that saved the same amount over the same period of time but got dramatically different results because of the rates of return they were able to make. No Mo' Broke people learn how to get a better return on their investments.

I always get two questions about that last example.

- ∞ Question One: Where can I get $200 per month to save?

- ∞ Question Two: Where can I possibly get those kinds of returns?

You probably already have the money.

Answer to Question One
(Where do I get $200 to save?):

In 2009, 75 percent of taxpayers got refunds. The average tax return is $2,900 or $240 per month. You probably already have the money available to save if you are part of that 75 percent.

If you are not in the 75% bracket who get a refund:

You will have to find a way to cut back on some things in order to save. For the average household, this means finding no more than a 5 percent savings. Cutting your expenditures back 5 percent will, in all likelihood, do the trick if you are part of the 25 percent that does not get a refund.

Answer to Question Two
(Where do I get those rates of returns?):

There are quality mutual funds with long track records that have averaged a 12 percent rate of return over the last 35 years.

To find a quality mutual fund, you can:

1. Research them yourself.

2. Use a financial service representative who will make suggestions for free but collect a commission from your transaction.

3. Use a financial advisor who will give you that advice for a fee.

It's Not Magic. It's Math.

A little saved consistently over a long period of time can make you a millionaire.

$200 per month for 35 years invested @ 3 percent = $148,000

$200 per month for 35 years invested @ 6 percent = $286,000

$200 per month for 35 years invested @ 12 percent = $1,100,000

You can retire with a million dollars!

A modest amount invested consistently over a long period of time can turn into a substantial sum.

Is it guaranteed? No. Mutual funds carry some risk.

What *is* guaranteed is that if a person does not save wisely during his or her working years, that person will be broke during their retirement years.

Developing the Skills

Part of the reason so many of us struggle with money and having enough of it is because we have never really taken the time to consider the cost. That is, we don't understand the real cost of the things we buy. We don't understand our financial life cycle. We don't understand the power of compound interest and how it can work for us or against us. And last but not least, too many of us fail to consistently plan how we are going to use our money. Most of us know what happens to those who fail to plan. They simply fail. A **budget** is the key to a good plan.

A Good Budget

A Budget Is a Plan for Your Money

A budget is a plan for our money and should be made at least monthly. The first few months of using a budget can be difficult, because most of us are going to forget to include important items. However, this is no excuse to quit trying. Stick with it and within 6 months, you will become proficient. You will become world-class after a year of practice.

Key 2: Consider the Cost

Budget Keys

- ∞ The budget should be written down and not merely kept in one's head.

- ∞ If married, one partner may draft the budget, but the other must look at it and have a real say on changes.

- ∞ The budget will never work if one spouse bullies the other spouse into a budget. Both parties must have a full say and be in agreement.

- ∞ A budget must include ALL income and expenses.

- ∞ Once the budget is made, it is law.

Practice Makes Perfect

It takes time to get the budget right. The first few months my wife and I worked on the budget, we invariably left off important items that really messed up our plans.

However, the more we did it, the better we got. It may take 6 months or longer to master budgeting.

Budget Tools

- ∞ There's nothing magic to it. A sheet a paper, a pencil, and a pen are all that are needed.

- ∞ There are many free budget worksheets and spreadsheets available.

- ∞ Most computer spreadsheet programs come with a free budget template to help you get started.

The next few slides go over some sound budget guidelines for a No Mo' Broke life.

Starter Budget

About the Starter Budget

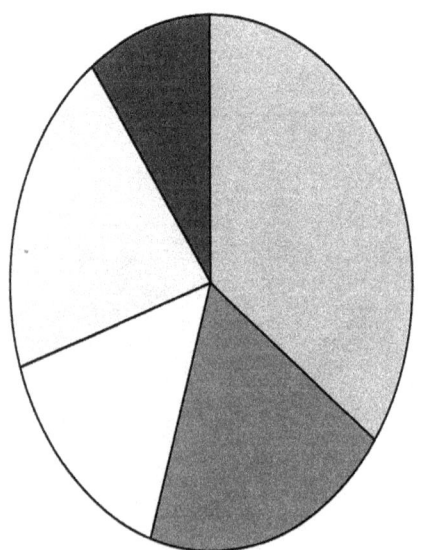

STARTER BUDGET
"Get on the Road to No Mo' Broke"

- 35% Housing
- 20% Transportation
- 15% Debt
- 20% Other
- 10% Savings

The starter budget category percentages were taken from the advice of a leading financial services company.

Based on their experience with their millions of customers, they know folks cannot succeed financially if they get too far outside these targets.

The starter budget targets fall short of No Mo' Broke targets, but are the minimal required in order to have a sustainable budget. In other words, if the amount you spend goes beyond these guidelines, you will likely have something go wrong and end up in the hole financially (that is, end up going ***deeper*** into debt).

- ∞ No more than 35 percent on all housing-related expenses

  Net Pay/Take-Home Pay (what's on your check) x .35 = the most you can spend on all housing-related expenses (rent or mortgage, utilities, taxes, insurance, and upkeep).

- ∞ No more than 20 percent going to transportation expenses

  Take-Home Pay (what's on your check) x .20 = the amount you can spend on transportation (gas, maintenance, taxes, insurance, finance charges, and depreciation).

- ∞ No more than 15 percent going to debt service beyond one's mortgage.

  Take-Home Pay x .15 = the most you can spend on other debt payments (credit cards, student loans, and the like).

- Save 10 percent

    Take-Home Pay x .10 = the amount saved for retirement, college, emergencies, and special goals).

- 20 percent for everything else

    Take-Home Pay x .20 = amount that can be spent on everything else (food, clothing, entertainment, health care not already taken out of one's check, and offerings and charitable giving).

Starter Budget Problems

The starter budget is not where we want to be. It assumes we will always have debt.

Further, it fails to give back to God. Christians nationally give less than 3 percent of their income. In underfunding the churches, we greatly limit the good that can be done. (More on that later.)

The starter budget cannot be our final budget. No Mo' Broke people give better and live better than that.

Transitional Budget
"Make small changes to become a giver"

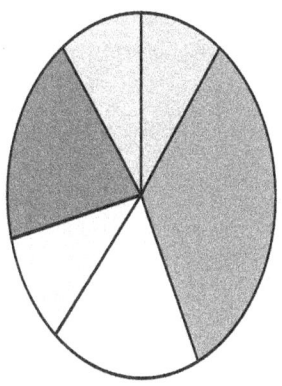

☐ 10% Tithes	■ 33% Housing	☐ 18% Transportation
☐ 10% Debt Services	■ 19% Other	☐ 10% Savings

∞ Starts tithes of 10 percent.

∞ Reduces nonhome-, nonauto-related debt service by 1/3 (or 5 percent of the total budget) to get debt service down to 10 percent of income.

∞ It squeezes 5 percent-10 percent savings out of the other categories to allow for tithes.

Savings are initially used for a rainy-day fund and insurance, if needed.

Transitional Budget Points

- 10 percent tithes

    Net Pay/Take-Home Pay x .10 given to your church (or charitable institutions if you take a less literal view of biblical teaching).

- No more than 33 percent on all housing-related expenses

    Net Pay/Take-Home Pay (what's on your check) x .33 = the most you can spend on all housing-related expenses (rent or mortgage, utilities, taxes, insurance, and upkeep).

- No more than 18 percent going to transportation expenses

    Take-Home Pay (what's on your check) x .18 = the amount you can spend on transportation (gas, maintenance, taxes, insurance, finance charges, and depreciation).

- No more than 10 percent going to debt service beyond one's mortgage

Take-Home Pay x .10 = the most you can spend on other debt payments (credit cards, student loans, and the like).

- Save 10 percent

    Take-Home Pay x .10 = the amount saved for (retirement, college, emergencies, and special goals).

- 19 percent for everything else

    Take-Home Pay x .19 = the amount that can be spent on everything else (food, clothing, entertainment, health care not already taken out of one's check, and offerings and charitable giving).

No Mo' Broke Budget

Give More. Save More. Live More.

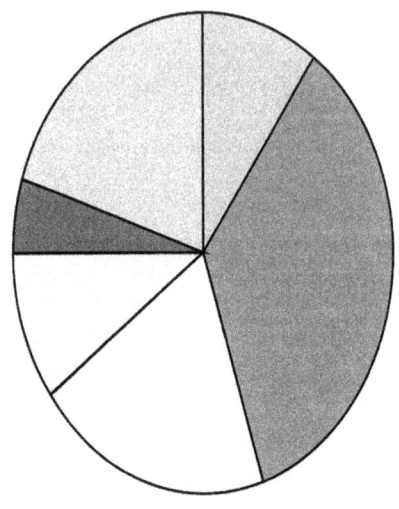

- 10% Tithes
- 20% Transportation
- 5% Special Goal Savings
- 35% Housing
- 10% Retirement Savings
- 20% Other

No' Mo' Broke Budget Target

∞ Eliminates all nonhousing-related debt and nontransportation-related debt.

∞ Saves for special goals beyond retirement and college savings.

∞ Permits us to spend a little more in the areas of housing, transportation, and other areas compared to the transitional budget.

No Mo' Broke Budget Points

∞ 10 percent tithes

Net Pay/Take-Home Pay x .10 given to your church (or charitable institutions if you take a less literal view of biblical teaching).

∞ No more than 35 percent on all housing-related expenses

Net Pay/Take-Home Pay (what's on your check) x .33 = the most you can spend on all housing-related expenses (rent or mortgage, utilities, taxes, insurance, and upkeep).

∞ No more than 20 percent going to transportation expenses

Take-Home Pay (what's on your check) x .20 = the amount you can spend on transportation (gas, maintenance, taxes, insurance, finance charges, and depreciation).

- ∞ 5 percent Special Savings Goals

    Take-Home Pay x .05 = the money you set aside for special goals (trips, furniture).

- ∞ Save 10 percent

    Take-Home Pay x .10 = the amount saved for (retirement, college, emergencies, and special goals).

- ∞ 20 percent for everything else

    Take-Home Pay x .20 = the amount that can be spent on everything else (food, clothing, entertainment, health care not already taken out of one's check, and offerings and charitable giving).

A Few Words about Cars and Budgets

For those of us who love the "new car smell," beware. The car is one of the biggest budget busters. Remember, we have 20 percent of the budget to spend on all transportation-related expenses. For a family that takes home $4,000 per month:

$$\$4,000 \times .20 = \$800$$

This amount includes gas & upkeep, title and tags, insurance, finance charges, and depreciation. AAA has the most complete information on this I have found. Through a Web search you can too. This can help you figure more precisely the real cost of a new vehicle. A good round number for a new vehicle is that it cost about 55 cents per mile. If you drive 15,000 miles a year:

15,000 x .55 = $8,250 per year, or $687.50 per month.

In this example, a family could afford to buy a new car and have a little leftover ($800 - $687.50 = $112.50) to afford the limited use of an older, paid for second vehicle.

Car Myth 1: "It is cheaper to drive a new car than an old one."

The 55-cents-a-mile cost of driving a new car should quickly dispel this notion. However, think of it this way. The average new car payment is around $300 per month, or $3,600 per year. For that much money, I could: have my transmission rebuilt every year (I paid $2,500 a couple of years ago), get a new set of tires ($500 which I purchased this year), pay for a year's worth of oil changes ($160), pay for roadside assistance for two cars ($150), and still have money left over!

Car Myth 2: "I always have a car payment."

Well, maybe—if you choose to do so. But consider the cost. Three hundred dollars per month invested @ 9 percent rate of return for 35 years = $846,449.

Would you rather have that new car smell or an extra $800,000 in your nest egg?

Driving older, paid for vehicles and investing what you would have spent on car payments can easily get you an extra two hundred or three hundred thousand dollars over the course of your working life if you are starting later. It is not at all unrealistic to accumulate an extra million dollars for someone who starts early.

Key 3: Pay God First

You have heard it said, "Pay yourself first," but a Christian believes that our Creator comes first in all things. No Mo' Broke Christians give back to God our firstfruits. Here is why:

- ∞ It helps makes us the type of people God wants us to be.

- ∞ It allows the church to do the work God wants us to do.

The habit of paying God first helps us develop the self-discipline needed to live the lives God has call us to live.

Why do we need to tithe?

Matthew 6:21 says: *"For where your treasure is, there your heart will be also."*

Being generous and joyfully dedicating the first tithes or fruits of our labor to God helps to create a heart inclined to God.

Why pay God first?

It makes the work of the Church possible.

Why do we need to tithe?

Malachi 3:10 says: *"Bring the whole tithe into the storehouse, that there may be food in my house."*

The tithe makes the work of the church possible. Everyone has a right to make sure the church is a good steward of its resources. Everyone has a responsibility to tithe.

What could your church do if it had the money?

Key 3: Pay God First

- ∞ Christians nationally give less than 3 percent of their income to the church. That's less than a third of what they should be giving.

- ∞ What kind of work could your church do if it had three times the budget to do it?

- ∞ How many lives could be changed, families fed, children educated, and neighborhoods transformed if the church had sufficient income?

- ∞ The churches have a responsibility to use the money in a way that empowers. Christians have a responsibility to give.

Why Pay God First?

Self-Discipline

Lastly, I have never met a person who could not live on 90 percent of their income who could live on 100 percent. Tithing helps us develop the self-discipline we need to be successful.

How To Tithe:

- ∞ We give 10 cents of each dollar we take home. Net Pay/Take-Home Pay (the amount of your check) X .10.

- ∞ For example, if you take home $1,600 per month:

    $1,600 X .10 = $160 = monthly tithe

- ∞ We get to use 90 cents of each dollar to take care of our households.

    $1,600 x .90 = $1,440 = the amount you get for your budget.

Key 3: Pay God First

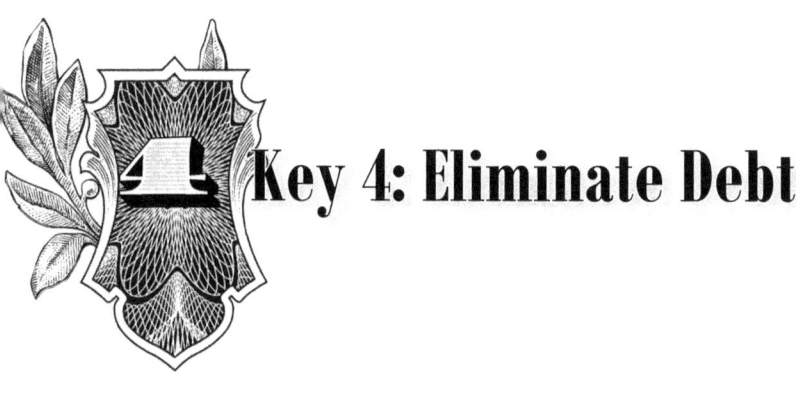

Key 4: Eliminate Debt

Proverbs says that the borrower is slave to the lender.

Do you feel like you are working hard but have nothing to show for it? Do you feel like a hamster stuck on a wheel? Are the bill collectors hounding you and robbing you of your peace? Are your bills taking everything from you? Eliminate debt and get your life back.

Keys to Eliminating Debt:

- ∞ When in a hole, stop digging.

- ∞ Pay off the mortgage within 20 years. No more than 35 percent of income on housing-related expenses, including the mortgage.

- ∞ No more than $20,000 of debt for an undergraduate degree.

- ∞ Use a snowball approach to eliminate debt.

When in a hole, stop digging.

Stop Digging: No New Debt.

Our household went two Mississippi summers without air conditioning in our bedrooms because we were committed to not adding to our debt. This past summer, having saved what we needed for new heating and cooling units, we paid cash (and got a great deal). Sometimes it just comes down to making a choice that the cycle has to stop. Sometimes it means short-term pain for a long-term gain.

Avoid Becoming "House Poor"

- ∞ A home can be a great blessing, but only if we can afford it.

- ∞ If our expenses for mortgage, interest, taxes, utilities, and upkeep exceed 35 percent, then it is too much and we have become house poor.

- ∞ Work to pay off the home in 20 years rather than 30.

- ∞ Renters can use the same 35 percent number for their housing expenses. However, if your goal is home ownership, cut back that 35 percent and save the difference toward a large down payment.

Housing in Expensive Cities

There are a handful of major metropolitan areas where that 35 percent number is difficult to meet because housing costs are so high. In these cases, one has to make reductions in other expense areas, such as transportation. Many of these high-cost areas have great public transportation.

You may have to consider having a roommate or renting out part of your house or apartment. That's how my grandmother was able to buy her home. She used a bedroom and living room and rented out the other bedrooms (and attic and basement too!). Everyone shared the kitchen and bathrooms with very strict rules. It was only temporary.

The difference should not come out of your giving or savings category. Failing to give robs God and your fellow neighbor. Failing to save robs yourself and your family.

Student Loan Debt

A formal education is one of the most important things a person could have. Getting a degree can also dramatically increase one's earning potential. However, one should not come out of school crippled with debt.

Student Loan Debt Limits

Student loan debt should be limited to less than $20,000 for an undergraduate degree. And less than a total of

$50,000 for an advanced degree. If your advance degree is in a low-paying field (or fields with low starting salaries) such as: social work, journalism, child care, nonprofit or church work, **_stick to the $20,000 limit for both your four-year degree and your professional degree_**.

The loan repayment schedule should be no more than 10 percent of your expected income once you complete your education. Be realistic. Do your own research. Talk to people in your prospective field. Find out how likely you are to find work in your field and in your area. Learn what that work would likely pay you **_before_** taking on a pile of student loan debt.

If you are looking at more than $20,000 of debt as an undergraduate or more than $50,000 for a graduate degree, consider a less expensive school or program or paying as you go.

There are many people with both four-year- and advanced degrees who are miserable because they are drowning in debt.

Other Debts:
Are to be shunned and avoided.

Debt for depreciating assets such as cars, trucks, motorcycles, RVs, boats, campers, trailers, furniture, consumer electronics, and the like, is one sure way to stay broke. High-interest unsecured debt on credit cards and the like puts one in the express lane to being and staying broke.

Eliminate Debt
Using the Snowball Approach:

1. Create a list of all of your debts: credit cards, car loans, student loans, etc., excluding your first mortgage.

2. Next to each one, write down the total balance owed.

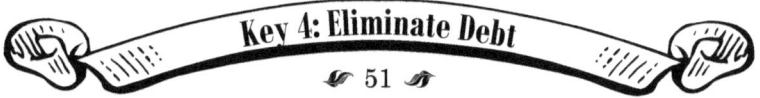

3. Reorder these from smallest to largest debts.

4. Pay the minimum payment on all of the debts except the smallest one.

5. Any extra money you can squeeze out of your budget goes toward paying off the smallest debt.

6. Celebrate your accomplishment when you get that first debt paid off.

7. Take the amount you were paying toward the first debt and put it toward the next smallest debt. Do this until this one is paid off.

8. Repeat steps six and seven until each debt is paid off!

Snowball Your Money to Eliminate Debt

As you pay off your smallest debt, roll that money into the next largest, and the next largest until you have a giant snowball of money crushing and wiping out your debts.

Debt Reduction Calculator

A debt reduction calculator to assist you in setting up your debt snowball and determining your debt freedom date can be found at:

www.vertex42.com/Calculators/debt-reduction-calculator.html

Key 5: Prepare for the Unexpected

It's going to rain. Lightning will strike. The furnace is going to go out. The car is going to break down. The kids are going to get sick. We are going to miss work to see about a family member. We are going to have to travel on short notice. A $2,500 rainy-day fund prepares us for the unexpected.

Read what the Bible says about being prepared.

The Parable of the Ten Virgins
Matthew 25:1–10

At that time the kingdom of heaven will be like ten virgins who took their lamps and went out to meet the bridegroom. Five of them were foolish and five were wise. **The foolish ones took their lamps but did not take any oil with them.** The wise ones, however, took oil in jars along with their lamps.

The bridegroom was a long time in coming, and they all became drowsy and fell asleep.

At midnight the cry rang out: "Here is the bridegroom! Come out to meet him!"

Then all the virgins woke up and trimmed their lamps.

The foolish ones said to the wise, "Give us some of your oil; our lamps are going out."

"No," they replied, "there may not be enough for both us and you. Instead, go to those who sell oil and buy some for yourselves."

But while they were on their way to buy the oil, the bridegroom arrived. The virgins who were ready went in with

him to the wedding banquet. And the door was shut.

Don't Miss the Feast

How many of us miss out on the wedding feast because we were not ready for the unexpected? You see, *life* has a great big "If" in the middle of it. No Mo' Broke means being prepared for life's ifs. Jesus also teaches us the spiritual principle, "Be ready in season and out of season." That spiritual principle is also a very sound financial principle. In order to live a No Mo' Broke lifestyle, we have to prepare for the unforeseen and unexpected.

Set A Little Oil Aside

Good Preparation Includes:

- ∞ Rainy-Day Fund of $2,500.

- ∞ Term-Life Insurance of 8 to 10 times each wage earner's income.

- ∞ Be sure to cover the stay-at-home spouse for at least 50 percent of the amount of the primary breadwinner's coverage (on the same policy).

- ∞ Cover children for an amount necessary to meet final expenses, around ($7,000) on the same insurance policy.

Life Insurance

Life insurance should be 20-year level term with a level premium (meaning the amount you pay never goes up) and face amount (meaning your benefit amount does not change during the life of the policy). The policy should be guaranteed renewable if you can afford it. (This means you will be able to renew the policy if you want, regardless of your health status.) Your spouse and children should be included on the same policy.

Group term insurance (insurance purchased though work) should be thought as a supplement to one's own policy. Group term insurance is not portable. When one leaves the job, one leaves the term coverage. In the meantime, a person may have become uninsurable. Therefore, each person or family should have their own term insurance policy in place. One may consider a permanent policy (if one would like) only after all other budget areas are being met. The premiums should come out of the 20 percent all-other-budget category. However, if a person follows the No Mo' Broke financial lifestyle, they likely will not need life insurance after 20 years. You will be able to self-insure.

Key 6: Prepare for the Future

- ∞ Retirement Fund (10 percent saved in an IRA, 401k, or some other savings vehicle)

- ∞ Emergency Fund (3–6 months of income)

- ∞ Special Goals Fund (for houses, autos, furniture, vacations, children's education, other major purchases)

- ∞ Have a Long-Term Care Program in Place

Long-Term Savings

After you have your term life insurance and $2,500 rainy-day fund in place, your next goal is to work your way up to saving 15 percent of your income every month.

Ten percent of your net income/take-home pay (what you get on your check) should be applied toward your retirement fund. If you are saving through a 401k or 403b, the contribution you have taken out is around 7 percent of your gross pay, which will equal around 10 percent of your net pay.

Another way to save for retirement is through an Individual Retirement Account (IRA). A person may contribute up to $5,000 per year. For a couple, that is $5,000 apiece. There are two types: Traditional and Roth. A Traditional IRA allows you to deduct your contribution from your taxable income (effectively allowing you to save more). A Roth IRA gets no up front tax deduction (but means you have to pay no taxes on the money when you are retired). Which one's better is a matter of opinion. Most financial professionals like the idea of not paying taxes on their retirement savings. Some prefer the idea of having a larger amount of money to invest over a longer period of time.

If you are on the fence about what you prefer, my advice is this: If you get a tax refund now, save in a Roth IRA. If you find yourself paying taxes, saving in a Traditional IRA may be a better choice. (Check with a tax professional.)

Five percent of your net pay should go toward your emergency fund. An emergency fund is different from a rainy-day fund and should not be touched except in the case of extreme financial hardship, such as the loss of a job or a serious family illness.

Fund money should be kept in a savings account or a money market. Make sure you understand the risks before putting savings in a money market account. Do not be concerned about getting a high rate of return from your emergency fund. Your goal is to have the money safe and readily available should a crisis arise.

After your emergency fund is fully funded, apply the 5 percent toward your special goals. This can include college savings for the kids, vacations, furniture, consumer electronics, and renovations to the house.

Pause your special goal saving to rebuild rainy-day and emergency funds if those funds are ever used.

Long-Term Care

Those over 50 should strongly consider putting a long-term care policy in place. Almost 50 percent of seniors will need additional care at home or care in a nursing facility. These costs can be enormous ($30,000 to $70,000 per year) and can quickly deplete one's nest egg. Long-Term Care (LTD) policies go up in cost. Take care of your other priorities first. However, if there is any way you can reasonably afford it, put a LTD policy in place.

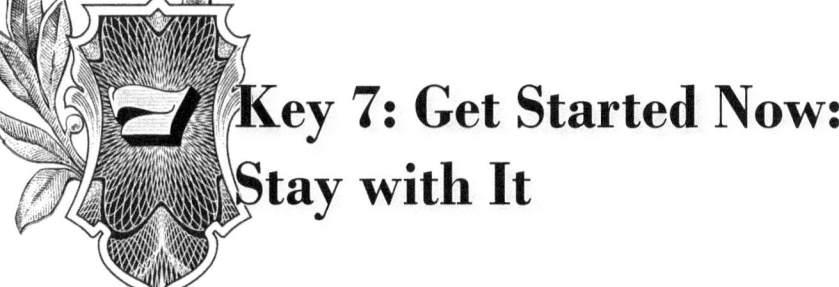

Key 7: Get Started Now: Stay with It

The stakes are very high. We are all responsible to be good stewards of our resources. Life will hold us accountable if we are not.

Matthew 25:27–29

Well then, you should have put my money on deposit with the bankers, so that when I returned I would have received it back with interest.

- ∞ So take the bag of gold from him and give it to the one who has ten bags. For whoever has will be given more, and they will have an abundance. <u>Whoever does not have, even what they have will be taken from them</u>.

Don't be that servant who did not take care of what was entrusted to him.

Make Time Your Friend

A person who managed to save $10,000 before he was 30 years old and invested that money at a 12 percent rate of return would have earned $528,000 by the time he was 65 (even if he had never saved another penny). A person who waits until they are 30 to start saving and investing $1,000 per year for the next 35 years at that same rate of return would only have saved $483,000. Thus, the second person who saved three and a half times as much would have less than the first person who started early!

On Your Own Or With Help

You have the tools you need to get started on your own.

There are many good people and companies who can help. If you would like a complimentary confidential financial analysis for you that will give you a debt freedom date and a retirement savings goal, email your name, address, and phone number to the address below. They will also calculate the amount of the life insurance you need, as well as the size of the emergency fund you need.

myplan@nomobroke.net

The Time To Start Is Now!
You *Can* Win!

You Can Be No Mo' Broke!

www.ingramcontent.com/pod-product-compliance
Lightning Source LLC
Chambersburg PA
CBHW071749040426
42446CB00012B/2503